THE GO-GETTER HANDBOOK

5 Lessons to Help You Confidently Accomplish Your Goals

Written by Latoya Jean

The Go-Getter Handbook

Copyright © Latoya Jean, 2018

Cover image: © Danny Media

Published by Chocolate Readings via KDP Publishing

www.chocolatereadings.com

ISBN-13: 9781724475671

Publisher's Note

Printed and bound in the United States of America. All rights reserved. No part of this book may be reproduced or transmitted in any form or by any means, electronic or mechanical, including photocopying, recording, or by any information storage and retrieval system except by a review who may quote brief passages in a review to be printed in a magazine, newspaper, or on the Web without permission in writing from Latoya Jean.

Although the author and publisher have made every effort to ensure the accuracy and completeness of information contained in this book, we assume no responsibility for errors, inaccuracies, omissions, or any inconsistency herein. The advice and strategies contained herein may not be suitable for your situation. You should consult with a professional where appropriate. Neither the publisher nor the author shall be liable for damages arising here from.

Dedication

I am dedicating the Go-Getter handbook to all the strong, independent, women out there who are working hard to succeed in life. The strength of a woman lies in how she is able to rise above everything that was meant to destroy her. Always remember that you are beautiful and that there is both pain in beauty and beauty in pain. Rise from the ashes and know that there IS a God that loves you dearly and unconditionally.

Love Always,

L. Jean

Table of Contents

Introduction	7
Aspirers	13
Go-Getter Quotes	17
The Doers	19
Go-Getter Quotes	25
The Indecisive	27
Go-Getter Quotes	33
The Detractors	35
Go-Getter Quotes	43
The Motivators	45
Go-Getter Quotes	55
Conclusion	57
About the Author	59

Introduction

As the 21st century evolves, women are becoming more dominant and branching out in every aspect of life. At one point, being a business owner was only for highly educated or financially stabled women. The statement commonly used is "born in the money or married to the money". These are women who marry someone who is wealthy, or those born into wealthy families. Women have now dominated above and beyond what they have imagined or dreamed of. Whether it is balancing a stable home, providing for their family, looking fabulous, maintaining their health or managing their personal relationships, women are going after what they want in life.

Due to women being more ambitious, the evolution of a go-getter has manifested. So, what exactly is a go-getter? A person who seeks, aspires, and develops the necessary steps to accomplishing a particular set of goals.

Not every woman has the same drive or mindset to step out on faith and do what they want. Hope is not a strategy, we cannot hope to be better or do better, and we simple have to plan to be better.

You should be relentless in pursuit of your goals, be unstoppable and the universe will open up and release everything that you crave for.

Over the years, I have identified myself with women who simple have the drive, the mindset, the will, and the ideas - but never the will to execute them. In this handbook, I have identified five types of women, as well as how they influence us in our daily lives.

For some women, their ambition is always to do or become something more; these are the **Aspirers.**

Whilst for some it's taking action and making steps to achieve success; these are the **Doers.**

The other category falls into uncertainty. Their favorite phrases are: but; the kids, school, the job, my age, the, the….

These types of women always have some excuse, the **Indecisive.**

Unfortunately all women are not go-getters. There are women that make the negative comments, seek to annihilate, discourage and destroy the three types of women listed above either through relationships with family; friends, associates or partners. These women are the **Detractors.**

And lastly, there is a type of woman that comes out in every country, age group, ethnicity, social background, work or play. The type of woman who speaks life into your movement, your struggles, your pain, and your dreams; she is the **Motivator.**

The five different types of women that are mentioned are truly evident in today's society. As a woman, your goal is to evaluate yourself, your life, your environment, your friends, and your associates. Don't be afraid to ask yourself: *Where do I want to be? How do I plan on getting there?*

Every single step of fulfilling ones greatest potential begins with *you.* Yes, you the individual. The minute you choose to do what you really want to do, you actually start living a different kind of life. The life you truly want.

Every successful woman that you emulate or see on the cover of magazines, on billboards, motivational speakers, CEO's, business owners, career women, women who are making waves, all had one thing in common: they had a vision. They had dreams, which developed into plans and with small and attainable steps – these women set their mind on achieving them.

Success does not come over night; it takes hard work, determination, discipline, trials, failures and even more attempts to accomplish the goal. What sets you above and beyond the rest is the willingness to keep afloat and persistent towards achieving what seems unachievable.

As a Go-getter asks yourself: what is my purpose? Where do I want to be? What tools do I need to utilize and who are the people I need to meet and associate with to help me bring this dream to life?

These questions will be the start of a new journey. On the following pages, you will find parables to help you identify with the women who have similar stories to your own. Think of yourself as you read the stories and be motivated to become the woman you were destined to be: a true Go-getter.

Aspirers

~Hopes & Ambitions~

Linda had always dreamt of owning her own business. She loved fashion and wanted to be a fashion designer. She grew up in the suburbs and there wasn't anything fashionable there, except for the old buildings that painted the streets of her town. The clothes that she saw and wore were nothing notable, or even close to the fashion she saw in the magazines and dreamt of wearing one day. She went to college and did basic fashion designing. There were not many clothing stores in her town, so she settled for a job in a convenient store as a clerk. Oh how Linda dreamt of moving to New York! *Things* happen in New York.

Linda would get a few outdated magazines sent to the store for sale. She would read stories of designers, the type of clothes that they made and wore. However, she has never gotten the chance of taking a trip out of town or following her long felt dream of moving and starting her life in the Big A.

She still lived with her parents, and still occupied the room she had since she was a child. The only thing that changed was her bed, as she had outgrown the small, single bed her parents had gotten her. She had no children, but felt safe and comfortable with her parents; therefore the thought of moving away terrified her. How could she leave the safety of her home, her parents, and her room?

Linda was saving towards her dream, but she never thought of making the first move of seeing the city. Her random thoughts about her dream life included having a small apartment, a big cozy bed, maybe a small dog and a nice TV with an unlisted amount of channels to watch, and most definitely her sewing machine to get some work done and have them displayed. How could she do this? When will she make this move?

The best way that Linda could have helped herself was to take the first step towards achieving her goals. But before she could do this she had to move away from what was holding her back.

As females, we are drawn by emotions, some physical, mental, and physiological. Females are drawn to things such as life events, family, loved ones, loyalty to our jobs, our spouse, etc. What we need to move away from is our feelings, yes our feelings, of what is and what will be if we do this. When we process our thoughts; we have to act on them. We have to move from thinking to doing to fully understanding and be able to achieve that which we seek.

You will never know the outcome until you make that first step, have that first trial, and until success comes knocking. Then you can truly say: yes, I did it!

If Linda had made an attempt to move to New York with the little savings she had and tried to start the business at least she would have known if it would work or not.

She would have also been able to feel how it feels to fall down, lose or how to start over.

Experiences and bad days help to set us up for better days. Aspiring to do something without ever trying does not give us the results that we truly need.

A dream will forever be a dream if not placed into perspective. We also need to take the necessary steps to accomplish those dreams. If your desire to succeed is strong enough, then you will eventually find a way to accomplish your dreams.

Therefore, as an **Aspiring** woman, it is your goal to set tasks, goals, and the necessary procedures to attain what you thought or believed is only of the mind.

Martin Luther King once said, "If you think it, you can achieve it".

Believe this is so and act on yourself today. Not tomorrow, not next week or next month. The time is now.

Go-Getter Quotes

Be a doer, not a dreamer.

Success is not determined by your circumstances, it is determined by your decision.

When you have faith in yourself you can do anything you set your mind to.

Your thoughts leads to feelings, that leads to action that leads to results.

Never doubt yourself that is what haters are for.

The Doers

~A Radical Mindset Shift~

A **Doer,** as the word states, is a person who acts rather than talks or think; the mover, the ultimate actions of a Go-getter. **Doers** are persons who become actively involved in a project, works on it and ensure it is followed through in its entirety.

In life, with so many personal struggles and a world where people tend to pull each other down rather than build each other up, we have to be optimistic and see the good in the bad people, the bad people in the good, and the bad situations that can be turned into good outcomes. It is told that optimism is the one quality more associated with success and happiness than any other.

How can one be optimistic you may ask? By focusing on you as an individual; you do this by eliminating the bad thoughts, the negative attitude, and you remove yourself from the negative circles. Your ultimate goal is working on you. Do this by accomplishing self-actualization; this is when you come to the realization of your God-given talent and potentials, how you use and mind these determines how far you will go and the type of life you will live.

After self-actualization, you become the ultimate force ready and fit to achieve what seemed unattainable. A reminder - nothing in life is impossible. The word itself says "I AM Possible".

So after self-seeking and realization, you are on the road to achieving your goal, remember: "Success is a journey not the destination". In life, you don't wait for the perfect moment, take the moment as is and make it perfect.

Tanesha

Tanesha was working in the banking industry for over five years. She went to college and got her college degree in Financing. She had excellent customer service skills and ensured that the clients were well served. She would be happy to go to work each day, but did not feel fulfilled.

She was missing something. She wanted to do things on her own time and on her own terms. She had a dream, but how could she leave her consistent salary, her two weeks' vacation each year and her retirement at 65 with her pension?

All of the "if's" felt scary and she feared a little what would be. Then one day, she started to read and enlighten herself on creating her wealth from having the dream job she seeks, and doing things on her own time.

Tanesha tapped into her God-given purpose. She awakened her passion.

Are you in a similar situation as Tanesha? Do you find yourself wanting more, believe you deserve better?

Ask yourself: What could I do for myself that could create my dream job, give me more at home time with my family and unlimited vacation time?

The best decision Tanesha made was to begin educating herself, embracing her futuristic plans by asking herself 'how can I achieve this goal?'

When you tap into this element of changing your mindset and thoughts, then things begin to flow easily. I strongly believe that every woman has a talent, an ability, or a skill that she can tap into and create a profitable and substantial business to mine herself and take care of her family.

Greatness begins in the mind. If you want to be great, you have to shift your mindset. This was the best decision she made and this was the step she needed to get her to the place she was meant to be.

As a **Doer,** your number one goal is to truly believe in yourself. There's no other way to say this. With success comes time and perseverance. You have to be prepared to go through levels of defeat and failures. Your failures are what will push you through to the end.

Believe in your dreams and take action steps toward your goal; no matter how small, each small step brings you closer to the goal at hand. If you ever feel as if you want to give up, look back and see how far you have come and what you have achieved. This should be your motivator. Recognize every single accomplishment and celebrate them as you go along, you deserve it.

Go-Getter Quotes

Speak success over your life, family and business every day.

I expect to be successful in all my endeavors.

I am assertive, ambitious and always ready for the call of duty.

Determination and courage are my two strongest inner goals.

I will not back down or be defeated, God is in control.

The Indecisive

~Ambiguous Character~

Indecisiveness is a trait of women who are unclear or uncertain about what they want. This speaks to the women that have problems making good choices or making effective decisions. Women who are of this nature are hesitant to making decisions that relates to their well-being, their life goals or their success.

As women, we have to take the responsibility of knowing what we want and make the necessary steps to achieve such wants. There are two things that prevents us from taking those steps: fear and procrastination.

Fear often contains the greatest growth. Fear can either direct you towards something good, keep you tied up, or held back from achieving something great.

Fear is a product of our thoughts. It is something all successful people encounter. How you deal with your fears will set you above and apart from your peers and your competitors.

Procrastination can take hold on many aspects of life, having you feeling guilty, inadequate or leaving you in self-doubt.

Procrastination is also the fear of success. Sometimes we procrastinate because we fear what success will be like and what the results will be if we pursue it.

Success is a highly respected responsibility. Because **Indecisive** women do not know how they will handle their success, they tend to follow this trend. The only way to know if you will succeed is to start where you are. Once you begin, the possibilities are endless. Do not wait for a perfect moment, take your moment and make it perfect for you.

No more talking of what you are going to do, but start doing and being about what you want to do. Whenever you have a choice and don't make use of it, then obviously your choices will make you. By not making quality choices, you are setting yourself up for failure.

Tammi

Tammi had a love for make-up and hair care. She's been doing this type of work just for fun since she was thirteen years old. She was embracing her passion; helping to beautify others. What she didn't know was that this was her money maker; the job that would be the right fit for her. However, she got a job in the music business industry as a Road Manager for a popular music star.

Tammi's job function took her around the country meeting the big shots. Yet, she was tired of her role. As this job took away her nights and had her marketing during the day, her job duties started to represent one of a vampire lifestyle. She slept during the days, and had to work during the nights. *What next* she thought, *how can I get away from this lifestyle?* She felt the need to make a change so she did a six month beauty and hair care course during the days when she should be resting. She dreamt of a way out. She wanted a way out. So the first step she took towards her dream was to sacrifice some sleep so she could complete her course.

Tammi completed the course within the six months duration and passed with flying colors. She knew that she had this. Hey, it was her passion.

And what exactly is passion? An individual's passion is what you love to do, it is what you desire to do, and it is what takes you from being to doing.

For Tammi, she loved hair care. She wanted to make that her first choice, but even though she did her course, the fact of doing it professionally scared her. *How will people react if I don't give them the treatment they require? How will I start and where will I get the funds to start my own business?* All of these thoughts were continuously playing over and over in her head. And before she took the next step towards her passion, she sat in the same job for another two years doing what she didn't like.

People who are successful in life do not operate in their emotions. Get your heart out of it and your mind into it. First, you have to start by doing what's necessary. Next, you do what is possible, and suddenly you are doing the impossible, as quoted by Saint Francis.

The bottom line of achieving ones goal is to take the necessary steps to achieving them. The minute you choose to do what you really want to do, you'll start living a different life.

Go-Getter Quotes

I choose happiness, success and abundance in my life.

Ambition is the first step to success, action is the next.

Every day is a new day to create a new opportunity and take another step towards your goals.

Failures are bigger in my head than in reality.

Self-confidence is a feeling of trust in one's ability, qualities and judgments.

The Detractors

~Critics and Fault Finders~

Not everyone will cheer for you on your journey. And not everyone will support your goals. People tend to pretend well. Some will even laugh with you and act as if they are happy with you while you're working to accomplish your life goals. Just the mere thought that you might actually make it scares them. As soon as the bank notes start accumulating, people will start recognizing who you are. And the positive feedback that once rolled in will start rolling out.

Be happy for these types of people. While the deceit may be hurtful, it all adds to the upward mobility of your future. Do not let confusion and their deceit distract you or intimidate you. Their part of the process has just ended; their journey with you is no more. Do you see the evidence of their presence in your walk to fame? You needed them to push you and to cheer you on. Yes, that was the motivation you needed from the people you trusted or thought you could trust, but now that you have superseded their expectations, they find it no longer fit to be your friend.

This evaluation is evident in today's society. Unfortunately, you will have female friends who act as if they are your ride or die, but as soon as you start to get somewhere, they start hating. Just to be clear; they were hating from day one.

Envy is what kills them. They lack the necessary skills and desires that you have to get what you want and the drive to go with all their might and get things done. They didn't know you would be persistent. Heck no they didn't know you would get this far, because at the back of their minds they thought: *she does not have it in her; she does not have the resources, she is going to stop, etc.*

These types of people are the **Detractors**. Do not be heavily burdened or disheartened by their envy because this only seeps unhappiness in their own lives. Allow their envy to be your fuel to go and get it.

My mantra is "be happy for each and every one as we can all succeed." What will be your go-getter mantra?

I believe if we support and help each other, good energy from the universe will draw our individual success to us and it becomes a "win, win" for us all.

Maria

Maria grew up in a small community and went to a prominent high school. While attending, she met a friend during her freshmen year. They were drawn to each other. They had similar qualities and they became very good friends. The friendship continued all the way up into the 12th grade. It was now time for them to graduate high school. The dread and the fear of them being apart were evident.

They promised themselves that they would continue being friends. Regardless of the fact that they will now go on and live separate lives and attend different schools. They missed the weekends or days they could just walk by each other's house and have some play time, dress up in each other's clothes and just be the friends they loved being with each other. However, the time came and they were registered in different colleges away from each other. They still managed to communicate and met occasionally.

It happened that Maria's friend had to sit out of college for a year because her parents were having some financial difficulties and her school fees were not paid for the following school year. Maria dreaded the thought of her friend having to sit out of college for a year. She thought of the stress and anxiety that would be placed on her. *How could I help my friend*, she thought? Then she did the next big thing she knew she could do; she started to ask around in her community if anyone was hiring and could give her friend a job so she could save up some funds for school.

Maria finally got a positive answer from Mr. Brown, who owned a deli close to their home and she hurriedly went and told her friend. When she told her friend the news, she didn't seem excited, but she wanted to help.

Her friend didn't like the idea of working in a deli, oh no! "When my other friends come and see me here what will they think? That I am just a college drop out with no experience, so I had to settle for Mr. Brown's old deli," the friend stated.

Maria felt very disappointed and she said to herself, *well I tried,* and sadly went home.

Days would pass, and then weeks. She heard less and less from her friend. She cared for her and wanted the best for her. The summer holidays came and she went home to her community only to find out that her friend had migrated to another country to work on a Student Visa and didn't even tell her. *Oh, what a disappointment,* she thought. *I thought we were cool. She never said good bye.* She felt alone and heartbroken that the one friend she thought she had would disappear without saying good bye.

Four years passed and Maria completed her first degree in nursing and became a registered nurse. She met new friends. She even met a nice guy and they got married. She was happy. Still, she thought at times, *why did my friend leave without saying good bye?*

The moral of this story: people will come into your life to either make you or break you. What you decide to do from their actions determines your success. Also, you cannot help everyone. Not everybody will understand the drive you have in you to help them to achieve their own success.

Maria genuinely wanted to help her friend to get back in school and continue her studies. She loved her friend and wanted to help. The contrast, however, was her friend didn't need her help because she thought it was degrading.

In life, we have to take what we can get until we get what we truly want. It's not about where you are, but how you deal with your situations and work to better yourself and achieve your dreams.

Maria's friend left without saying goodbye because she envied her from day one. She was able to go full time and she wasn't. Envy is a friendship killer. Be careful of those who say they are happy for you, because not everyone who laughs with you actually means good.

Be careful of what you listen to, who you listen to; watch how they treat and react to you. The only distraction should be you, and because you have a purpose, then you are inclined with your purpose and your goals. So avoid all negativity and keep focused.

Go-Getter Quotes

Be willing to give, but only when you aren't expecting anything in return.

If the battle is not between you and your destiny, then it's a distraction.

Pray about your purpose so you don't end up pretending to be something you're not.

If you keep counting the steps you will never make it to your destination.

Let no one discourage your ambitious attitude, you don't need a fan club to achieve your goals. Be your own motivation.

The Motivators

~*Movers and the Shakers*~

To truly be motivated, one has to have the drive, a consistent determination to succeed or win at all cost. When one is motivated she is enthused about herself. **Motivation** comes from everything around you. How you accept and decipher this motivation is based on what you seek to achieve in your life.

Women hold so many titles in this world. First, imagine us bearing children, monthly menstrual cycle, discrimination of our skin, our hair texture, the way we talk; discrimination against our body structure. If we continue to search for validation from people, we will never achieve our goals or live a happy life.

We are more than what society says we are. We are more than how they perceive us to be. We are children of God; made unique and special in His image. We build societies, communities, and organizations.

So, just in case you forget, fix your crown and remind yourself of who you are. Eleanor Roosevelt said "A woman is like a tea bag, you can't tell how strong she is until you put her in hot water." This speaks volumes as it is speaking to the fact that our circumstances either pushes us or breaks us.

As a woman, I can safely state that we are too inclined to others and their thoughts about us, about how we live our lives, how we dress, the careers we choose, the type of business we operate and even the spouse we choose. Get over how they see you, what they think about you and be happy with who God says you are. You set the bar for your own expectations of yourself. As long as you're doing your best and coming from a place of love and kindness, your opinion of yourself is what truly matters.

Anything you have to deal with doesn't need a yes from anyone but God. At the end of the day, we could try all we can to please those around us and miss our calling, our God-given purpose. Think about it – then who would be happy? You or your friends? Snap out of people pleasing, it's all about you.

What goals do you have, what dreams do you have, when was the last time you've taken a vacation? You need to do you, have faith in yourself that you are talented enough, you are more than enough and you deserve everything good that God has in store for you. No one will walk up to you and give you handouts. You have to work hard for everything you need in life.

Your goals may seem unattainable at the moment, dreams unachievable, but with hard work and determination you can succeed.

What is success you may ask? For some people it means a lot of different things. I classify success as small progressive steps towards achieving a goal. Success is not so much the end product, but the journey. While others place a tangible item on success, I look at the steps you take towards your goals, no matter how small they are.

Sara

Sara was always a go-getter. Although she grew up in the hood, she got pregnant with her first child in high school and had to sit out for the last two years - she still had the mindset of a mover and a shaker. While she was unable to get her high school diploma, that did not stop her from pushing past her limits and doing well for herself.

Living her life as a single mom, she faced many defeats and many obstacles. She had no support from her parents, who denied her the love she needed when she got pregnant at age 16. How disgraceful it was for them that their little princess was about to be a mom. So to avoid the disgrace, they sent her to live with her grandmother in the suburbs.

Grandma was Sara's biggest supporter. She loved and cared for her grandchild. Sara moved in with her grandmother when she was just six months pregnant, her little bump hardly showing. Grandma made sure she ate properly, took her vitamins and had her regular doctors' visit. Months passed and it was time to give birth, there was no father, no parents, no friends, just the support of her loving grandmother.

Sara had a beautiful baby girl and she now truly understood how to love unconditionally. She loved her baby and decided that she was going to be the best mother she could possibly be. Her grandmother was a Godly woman; she prayed with her and regularly took her to worship at her local church. The baby grew gracefully and started to crawl around the house. She was a happy baby, and grandma helped her take care of her as well.

While grateful for the help of her grandmother, Sara, was not feeling too good about herself and her current situation. She wanted more for herself and her little family. She knew she could do something valuable with her life.

One afternoon while she was sitting on the porch with grandma, she said, "Grandma, I need some advice. I was thinking of going back to school and complete my high school diploma and then move on to college." Grandma's face lit up when she heard the good news. She always knew Sara had the will power, but she never tried to force her. She allowed her to make that cognitive decision on her own.

Grandma reassured Sara that she was there for her and will do all she could to see her goals being accomplished. She gave Sara a hug and she held on tightly to her grandmother as tears ran down her face. Other than having her daughter, she hadn't felt this embrace from a parent figure in a long while. She loved her grandmother and promised to do everything to make her proud.

Sara started school and was doing well. She got a job in the afternoon while grandma watched after the baby. Time went by and Sara was progressing and doing very well for herself. Her baby was taken care of, and she was fulfilling her dream.

Four years later, Sara was graduating college with not only her diploma, but a degree in nursing. Her grandmother invited her parents to her graduation. They were smiling from ear to ear. Sara had mixed emotions. *Should I be happy, sad or upset?* She thought, but then she remembered the Godly principles her grandmother taught her. *After all, I was proving them wrong I exceeded their expectations,* she thought.

Life happens, things happen. We are all tested with negatives and limitations at times. It is how we deal with them that set us apart. All Sara needed was moral and emotional support. Thank God for her praying grandmother who kept her going during her difficult time. Now she had achieved a goal that may have seemed unattainable at the beginning, but that did not limit or stop her from pushing and accomplishing her goal. She pushed, she endured, and she conquered.

Sara had a vison, she had goals. Her having a baby at a young age didn't deter or stop her. She wanted to win and excel in life.

How many of you have a why? Why do you do what you do? Is it fulfilling, are you reaching your goals? Are you happy doing what you do?

This is an important self-evaluation. If you answered no to any one of those questions, then you need a change; a total transformation in who you are and where you want to be.

Just like Sara, you have to evaluate your current circumstances. She was her own motivation. A single, teenage mom that was underpaid; had no career, no high school diploma, a young daughter to support; a grandmother to make proud and parents to prove wrong. It is when we are pushed to our limits that we know how far we are capable of going.

We simply have to be our biggest motivation; we have to assess our situations. Ask yourself: *what is going on in my life that is not serving me or generating a purpose filled life?* As soon as you are able to do this, take the necessary steps to set yourself up for success.

As women, we are conditioned by our past and our environment. These are usually set factors that create our blueprints. For us to understand our blueprint, we have to understand our past mistakes, decisions, culture, religion and relationships. To create a positive life, we have to create and enable a positive mindset. Also, remember that your thoughts lead to feelings, which lead to actions, which leads to results.

We cannot play victim to our situations. Never act pitiful, and do not assume that your loss or mishaps are caused by anyone. You determine your faith by the decisions you make. In this life, you have to be brave and ready to stand up to anything that comes knocking at your door.

You have to challenge yourself every day to be better, work smarter and not harder, and think bigger. Your past is a good place to learn from, but never to live in. Look back, reflect, apply changes and move on.

Go-Getter Quotes

Never limit yourself, we live in a limitless world with endless possibilities, never say you can't and never give up.

It is not what we have in life, but who we have in life that matters.

Don't doubt yourself, work hard and make it happen.

Never judge people by their past, people change, people grow and people move on.

Nothing is hard for a woman who is determined to win.

Conclusion

I created this book so other women like myself can understand that your past does not define who you are. Your struggles do not limit you from becoming more than enough, and that we can be much more than what others limit us to be.

Use positive affirmations over your life every day. One of the number one secrets to living a successful life is having a positive self-esteem; believe you can do what you set out to do, believe that you deserve good things in your life and believe also that you will get it.

A Go-getter knows what she wants, believes in herself and makes the necessary steps to achieve her goals.

People may destroy or try to destroy your image, stain your personality, but they can't take away your character because no matter what you are admired by the people who really care.

Be grateful in everything and be thankful for your highs and your lows. Gratitude is very essential to your success; when you are truly grateful you will start to appreciate the simple blessings that you have in your life. You will also create a sense of contentment and accomplishment.

Just remember to be thankful in everything you do and help others along the way. Success is not measured by the amount of dollars you make, but the amount of lives you impact while you are alive.

About the Author

Latoya Jean was born and raised on the Island of Jamaica, graduating from Northern Caribbean University with a Bachelors in Management (2008). She has a loving family and has been blessed with 3 beautiful children. An avid lover of reading and writing, she expresses that love through her blog on her website, www.GoGetterMotivation.com. She is an entrepreneur at heart, venturing in various businesses including Life Coaching, Financial Consulting and Fashion Retailing. Latoya is very adventurous and loves to travel. She is a natural born philanthropist, sharing her light through service to others.

Made in the USA
Middletown, DE
29 January 2024

48452853R00035